Poetry Gems

Edited By Lottie Boreham

First published in Great Britain in 2017 by:

Young Writers
Coltsfoot Drive
Peterborough
PE2 9BF
Telephone: 01733 890066
Website: www.youngwriters.co.uk

SB ISBN 978-1-78820-984-7
Printed and bound in the UK by BookPrintingUK
Website: www.bookprintinguk.com
YB0316H

Foreword

Dear Reader,

Welcome to this book packed full of feathery, furry and scaly friends!

Young Writers' Poetry Safari competition was specifically designed for 5-7 year-olds as a fun introduction to poetry and as a way to think about the world of animals. They could write about pets, exotic animals, dinosaurs and you'll even find a few crazy creatures that have never been seen before! From this starting point, the poems could be as simple or as elaborate as the writer wanted, using imagination and descriptive language.

Given the young age of the entrants, we have tried to include as many poems as possible. Here at Young Writers we believe that seeing their work in print will inspire a love of reading and writing and give these young poets the confidence to develop their skills in the future. Poetry is a wonderful way to introduce young children to the idea of rhyme and rhythm and helps learning and development of communication, language and literacy skills.

These young poets have used their creative writing abilities, sentence structure skills, thoughtful vocabulary and most importantly, their imaginations, to make their poems and the animals within them come alive. I hope you enjoy reading them as much as we have.

Jenni Harrison

Contents

Edge Grove School, Watford

Natasha Bloom (5)	56
Dara Olunloyo (7)	57
Jessica Shah (6)	58
Bryony Sanders (5)	59
Fatemah Asaria	60
Aisha Lawton (5)	61
Yousuf Usmani (5)	62
Freddie Mills-Webb (5)	63
Ehije Izzi-Engbeaya	64
Oliver Cox (5)	65
India Bulmer (5)	66

Greenfield School, Woking

Saachi Rajani (6)	67
Austin Frith	68
Matthew Denison-Edson	69
Vikram Kurup	70
Myeesha Amani Zaki (7)	71
Meng-Yao Ai	72
Omar Elsharkawy	73
Harry Charlton (6)	74
Ruben Kalliopuska (7)	75
Inaya Kahn	76
Zachariah Placide-De-Horn	77
Jacob Jennings	78
Daniel Tate	79
Darragh Dailey (6)	80
Madeleine Chesher (7)	81
Mason Patrick Bartholomew (7)	82
Oscar Elam	83
Anna Lucia Stempel-Martinez (6)	84

Heather Avenue Infant School, Norwich

Lily Dolan (6)	85
Kara Rae Morgan (6)	86
Jake David Lofty (6)	87
Emilis Galdikas (6)	88
Kitty Clitheroe (7)	89
Joel Ruane (7)	90

Zaki Mokhbi (6)	91
Finn Harrison (7)	92
Mya-Rose Moss (6)	93
Tanvir Singh Rakkar (7)	94
Ella Cudden (7)	95
Ivy Jean Philbrock (5)	96

Meynell Community Primary School, Sheffield

Darcey Elizabeth Copley (6)	97
Majid Amponsem (6)	98
Amy Hobson (6)	99

New Leaf Inclusion Centre, Walsall

John Southhall (6)	100
Sophie Byrne (5)	101
Brayden Tyrese Francis (6)	102
Joshua Jay Till (6)	103

Oakhill School, Clitheroe

Francesca Brett (6)	104
George Purves (6)	105
Isabella Zappa (6)	106
George Crook (5)	107
Evan Black (6)	108
Elysia Blackburn (5)	109
Thomas Ashworth (6)	110
Orlaith Purves (6)	111
Caspar Cort (6)	112
Katie Hennighan (5)	113

Priorslee Academy, Telford

Chloe Isabella Greenway (6)	114
Sian Kaur Hothi (7)	116
Aditi Singla (6)	117
Freya Faye Harris (7)	118
Mahi Patel (6)	119
Eva Clayton (6)	120
Thomas Faulkner (6)	121
Brooke Smith (5)	122

James Frederick Atwell (6)   123

Scholar Green Primary School, Stoke-On-Trent

Hefin Salisbury (7)   124
Lily Viner (7)   125
Darcey Rose Yarwood (6)   126
Ethan Morris (6)   127
Lola Thornton (7)   128
Sally Beatrice Knight (7)   129
Darcie Gannon (7)   130
William Hough (7)   131
Roan Hercock (6)   132
Mara Taylor-Woods (7)   133
Dainton Skot Frost (7)   134
Nicholas Davies (6)   135
Molly Norbury (7)   136
Shaun Cavanagh-Frost (6)   137
Thomas Lewis (7)   138
Noah Cole (7)   139
Joseph Oliver (7)   140
Evie Potts (6)   141

St James Catholic Primary School, Millom

Lauren Thompson (7)   142
Bella Pedley (7)   143
Maya Clarke (6)   144

St John Of Beverley RC Primary School, Beverley

Martha Elizabeth Needler (6) 145

St John's CE Primary School, Sandbach

Sarah Gibson (6)   146
Lauren Jayne Ann Clorley (7) 147
Gemma Groves (7)   148
Oscar Alexander Forsyth (7)   149
Xanthe Williams (6)   150
Alyssa Calladine (7)   151

Jasmine Briggs (7)   152
Jeff-Lewis Cook (7)   153
Mieke Marie Douglas (7)   154
Iona Acir (7)   155
Amelia Mitchell (6)   156
Joseph Hollins (6)   157
Ruby Musgrave (6)   158
Archie Brennan (7)   159
Joseph Calladine (7)   160
Kaitlyn Clee (6)   161
Nicole Clee (6)   162
Caitlin Levitt (6)   163

Westwood Prep School, Oldham

Aasma Amna Khan (6)   164
Huzayfah Muhammad (6)   165
Muhammad Ismail (6)   166
Hannah Brown (6)   167
Fatimah AZ-Zahra Rasul (6)   168

Wood End Primary School, Atherstone

Jackson Haiden Sheahan (7)   169
Phoebe Hardwick (7)   170
Florence Rose Kinson (7)   171
Georgina Flavell-Dodson (7)   172
Olivia Schall (7)   173
Lily-May Connie Gleeson (7)   174
Lottie-Leigh Amiee Oattes (6) 175
Izabelle Maddison Carroll (7) 176
Euan Markgraaff (7)   177

Woodlea Primary School, Houghton Le Spring

Ava Dickeson (6)   178
Finley Pringle (7)   179
George William McDonald (6)   180
Jake Henry Shaw (7)   181
Beau Edith Gritton (6)   182
Amelia Kelsey (6)   183
Jasmine Slack (7)   184

Sophie Green (6)	185
Nathan Johnson (6)	186
Eleanor Hall (6)	187
Daniel Wells (6)	188
Lily Greenwood (6)	189
Grace Bell (7)	190
Oliver Dodsworth (7)	191
Antoine Turnbull (7)	192
Libby Bonner (6)	193
Jake O'Shaughnessy (6)	194
Matthew Warwick (6)	195
Caitlyn Allsopp (6)	196
William Anderson-Bell (5)	197
Ava Maddison (6)	198
Millie Lumsdon (6)	199
Jay Marlow (6)	200
Alfie Halliwell (5)	201
Jodie-Marie Corbett (5)	202
Freddie Temple (6)	203
Ethan James Suthern (5)	204
Jacob Patterson Brown (5)	205
Matthew Kelters (6)	206
Ben Richardson (6)	207
Violet Worrall (5)	208
Megan Bell (5)	209
Emelia Grace Hood (5)	210
James B Hudson (5)	211
Aaron Dye (6)	212
Oliver Nattrass (6)	213
Liam Snowball (6)	214
Ben Robinson (6)	215
Jaiden Basra (6)	216

The Poems

My Day At The Zoo

When I was two my Granny took me to the
zoo,
I skipped and I jumped when I saw the
camel's hump,
I ran and I squealed when I saw the hamster
wheel!
We went for ice cream and as we walked by
the stream,
I could hear the monkey's scream!
I dreamed of a lion that was so very hungry,
Gran said, 'Don't make him hungry Marcy!'
The zebra's stripes were very black and
white,
'Please exit through the gift shop there on
the right.'
I loved the cards at the gift shop and the
lovely animal teddies,
My day at the zoo made me so tired that
they reminded me of my bed-dy!

Marcy Ellis-Scarfe (5)

My Walking Companion To School

I imagined a giraffe named A-raffe
Dressed in an orange-brown patchy coat
And I in a blue-stripped coat
Side-by-side we walked along the London
streets to my school.

He was six and I was too, aged six years old
But he was 14 feet short
And I was 4 feet tall,
Side-by-side we walked along the London
streets to my school.

He could see up and I could see down,
I walked and talked all about the globe,
And all he talked the long lines of traffic to
school.
Side-by-side we walked along the London
streets to my school.

Time to cross the busy street to get across
the road,
I walked beneath A-raffe's long lean legs
like a zebra crossing.
Though many could miss me, none could
miss A-raffe.
Side-by-side we walked along the London
streets to my school.

I broke my fast with oats at home,
A-raffe munched on leaves all along the
way
On-time to school, breaking our fast with
breakfast.
Side-by-side we walked along the London
streets to my school.

I guide my pal into my classroom,
Thud! Knocked over!
Bent the rules and bent his neck to enter
the classroom,

Oh what a fun! A sight to see,
A-raffe along with the others –
Some like monkeys, some like lions, and others like bears
The animal safari was in the room.
As my teacher arrived, the rules came back to my memory,
A-raffe faded from my imagination and the distant hum off...
Side-by-side we walked along the London streets to my school.

Siddharth Raj Krishnamurthy (6)

Bee

I love bees because they make yummy
honey.
Honey is as sweet as chocolate and
sweeties.
Bears eat honey especially Winnie the Pooh.

Bees live in a habitat called a hive,
Each colony has a queen bee.
The bees help the plant to grow fruits.

Bees are as fast as a bolt of lightning.
If you harm them,
They can give you a powerful sting.
Bees are stripy like a tiger
So bye for now, I am a busy bee...

Naithan Jeyasiri

Penguins

Penguins can't fly but they can dive.
They catch fish which are alive.
Penguins slide on ice.
They are very very nice.
Penguins have chicks.
They sometimes have six.
Penguins live in snow.
The temperature there is quite low.
They huddle together to keep warm
In a big snowstorm.
Penguins come in different sizes.
The snow melts when the temperature rises.
The number of penguins is reducing
With the warmth global warming is producing.
The blanket of gases is getting thicker
and the penguins are reducing quicker.
From short to tall

We need to save them all.
We must stop the oil
From causing the big spoil.
We'll have to put the fish back
To save the penguin pack.
We must reduce, recycle, reuse.
We must do it now, there's no time to lose

Ahaan O (6)

Safari Zoo

One fun day I went to the safari zoo
Where all of my dreams came true

First I saw a fierce lion that looked very mad,
When we left his cage I was quite glad

We moved over to the giraffe that was so high,
His head seemed so tall like it was in the sky

Then we saw the elephants which were my best,
They were peacefully sitting taking a rest.

The gorilla was next in line to see
I did not want him to stand too close to me

The rhinos were the last animal we saw
But I wish there had been so many more

It was the best day and I had so much fun,
The magical zoo is where everyone should
come.

Alicia Sharma (6)

Whale Watching

I sit waiting
Watching the waves
Black and blue.

I sit waiting
Feeling the cold wind
Whistle and bite.

I sit waiting
Listening to the sea
Crash and splash.

I sit waiting
Then I see
Is that the whale?
'Yes,' says my Mummy.

I sit waiting
My eyes open wide
Then a big jump that tells me he's not
Going to hide.

I sit waiting
Then what do I see?
A big shoot of water
Much bigger than me!

Joseph Hibbert (6)

Wild Animals

Squirrels have bushy tails and whales swim in the sea happily.
Giraffes have very long necks and can reach very tall trees,
A snake hisses in the distance, here it comes.
And snails have slimy tracks behind its back.
Kangaroos can jump so high they can touch the tree tops.
Penguins can slide on their tummies on icy mountains.
Monkeys eat bananas all day long and have some fun.
Fishes are beautiful to see and can swim in the sea.

Maia Szczudlik-Bernard (7)

I Wish I Was An Animal

I wish I was an animal
I wish I was a swift kestrel swooping in the air
I wish I was an emperor penguin hugging my chicks
I wish I was a sporty jaguar sprinting in the rainforest
I wish I was a nosey duck that can waddle swim and fly
I wish I was a clever dolphin leaping the Pacific Ocean
I wish I was a cute guinea pig curled up on a lap.

Alexander Walker (6)

Beautiful Butterfly

B eautiful butterfly
U nder the flower she sleeps
T icking sound the butterfly wings make
T wirling in the sunshine
E veryone loves butterflies
R ainbows in the sky
F lutter the wings
L eaves fall down and down; bedtime
Y awning and yawning.

Isabella Darko (7)

The Flying Horse

I live on top of a cloud
Behind a waterfall.
I fly down to eat berries and flowers
And fly back up to paint the rainbows.

I see lots of birds and insects
I see children and smile at them
When they feel down, to make them smile
I fly back up to paint the rainbows.

Edward Evans (5)

The Scariest Lion

It's as scary as a werewolf
It eats like a piranha
It's as gold as treasure
It's as furry as a monkey
It's as mean as a tiger
It lives in Africa
It hunts like a tiger
It's as fast as a cheetah
Who am I?
I'm a lion.

Laith Farsi

The Marvellous Snow Wolf Of The Arctic

He is as fast as a chicken in a jetpack.

He eats like a tiger.

He hunts in a pack.

He is not pretty at all.

He howls at the night sky moon.

He is the dog family's leader.

His favourite food is ox.

Who is he?

He is a snow wolf.

Sy Farsi

Troubley Tiger - An Acrostic Poem

T eeth as sharp as brand new paper corners

I t likes to go to town, to eat fat lazy people

G rowls louder than a colossal sea wave

E nough to attack two rhinos alone

R ests in a deep, dark forest.

Arinjay Saha (6)

A Riddle

It can't fly as it has no wings,
It can't walk fast, only hops,
It swims with its flippers,
It has a black back, white tummy,
It slides on snow like a sleigh,
It is a bird, who eats fish,
It is my cute penguin.

Angelica Saha (6)

The Snake Is Awake

There was a snake who was quite scary
Who looked like he was hairy
He liked to go to the wood
And he was always so good
But he only came out during the light
Because he didn't like the night.

Nathan Kibby (5)

Horibl Naichr

(Horrible Nature)

Nature, why is there nature?
A pigeon, a pigeon just standing there
like a brute.
Get out of my garden!
Get away!
Aiaaaaaaaa!

Rory Bradley (6)

The Lion

Loud and scary lion roars
It has yellow fur and an incredible, brown mane
On the grass he likes sleeping
No! Don't touch the sharp, pointy teeth.

George Clarke

Arnold My Cute Fishy

F ast, he swims fast
I nteresting, he is interesting
S hiny, he is shiny
H ungry, he is hungry
Y et he is my favourite fish.

Benjamin Elliot Hammersley (6)

Untitled

C ats are fierce and they play and eat fish
A nd they have white fur and are happy
T ickle your cat.

Beren Tuana Karacam (7)

Love

I love you,
You love me,
You are an animal of the jungle,
I am a human of earth,
But love brings us together forever!

Aaria Bains (6)

Cat

C ats eat salty fish
A nd they chase mice
T errifying claws to eat with.

Johann Franck (7)

What Is It?

He is as cute as a seal
He is as good as a dolphin
He's a penguin.

Jake Rodway (6)

The Little Horse Rider

The butterflies were tap dancing
On the ears of my big white Lizzy, my horse.
Her hooves clip-clopping
up the track to the school.
Round and round we ride
until we are dizzy.

Jessica Gravestock-Whitaker (5)
Amberley Parochial School, Stroud

Kitten Sense Poem

Kittens taste rotten and hairy like hair.
Kittens taste of fluffy white kitten hair.
Kittens smell like hideous mud.
Kittens smell like trees.
Kittens look like fluffy, magnificent, black
and white beautiful beasts!
Kittens sound like miaow,
miaow like a baby lion.
Kittens sound like birds' sharp beaks.
Kittens feel smooth, furry
and silky like a piece of chocolate.

Emma Wood (6)
Corbridge CE First School, Corbridge

Kitten Senses Poem

Kittens taste like fluffy, hairy, warm,
squishy, soft meat!
Kittens smell fresh
and juicy like green grass!
Kittens look as white and fluffy as snow.
Kittens sound like purr, purr, purr,
like a shiver!
Kittens feel cuddly, soft, silky
and warm like a guinea pig.

Rose Versey (5)
Corbridge CE First School, Corbridge

Elephants Sense Poem

Elephants taste like dead hens!
Elephants smell like wind blowing
in the trees in the forest.
Elephants are like a monkey sitting
in the tree.
Broo, broo, broo like an elephant.
Elephants feel like soft, cuddly teddy bears.

Lucas Culverwell (5)
Corbridge CE First School, Corbridge

Dolphin Senses Poem

Dolphins taste of lots of stinky, rotting fish.
Dolphins smell like salty water.
Dolphins look like a blue and white beast.
Dolphins sound like a whale when
it wants its Mum.
Dolphins feel like a smooth whale.

Jemima Kate Greenley (6)

Corbridge CE First School, Corbridge

Rhino Sense Poem

A rhino smells like poo,
A rhino smells like wee!
A rhino looks grey.
A rhino looks like it's got a head.
A rhino sounds like a troll!
A rhino eats meat!
A rhino feels hard and grey.

Daniel Robert Marks (6)
Corbridge CE First School, Corbridge

Snake Sense Poem

Snakes taste of vile, smelly, slimy stomachs!
Snakes smell like slimy, vile meat and sick!
Snakes look like slimy, vile snakes!
Snakes sound as quiet as a snail.
Snakes feel like soft pillows!

Robbie Mitchell (6)

Corbridge CE First School, Corbridge

Crocodile Senses Poem

Crocodiles taste like wet fish.
Crocodiles smell like stinky fish.
Crocodiles look like scary wizards.
Crocodiles sound like a noisy car.
Crocodiles feel like a spiky pin.

Lucas Lennon Penny (6)

Corbridge CE First School, Corbridge

Donkey Senses Poem

Donkeys taste like grass and plants.
Donkeys smell like a red rose.
Donkeys look grey.
Donkeys sound like *clip-clop*.
Donkeys feel soft and fluffy.

Mia Metcalfe (5)

Corbridge CE First School, Corbridge

Tigers Sense Poem

Tigers taste like red meat.
Tigers smell like the fresh wind.
Tigers look like a hamster.
Tigers are louder than a dinosaur.
Tigers feels fluffier than a hamster.

Fred Irwin (5)
Corbridge CE First School, Corbridge

Puppies Sense Poem

Puppies, fast like dog treats.

Puppies, just like dog food.

Puppies smell like the perfume.

Puppies feel soft as a blanket.

Puppies sound like furry, furry sheep.

Ben Tiffin (6)

Corbridge CE First School, Corbridge

Cat Senses Poem

Cats tastes like cat food.
My cat smells like chicken.
My cat looks very black.
Miaows like a fluffy kitten.
My cat feels soft and cuddly like a donkey.

Isabella Quigley (6)

Corbridge CE First School, Corbridge

Dragon Senses Poem

A dragon tastes like fire.
A dragon smells like a fire.
A dragon looks like a fiery beast.
A dragon sounds like a fierce dinosaur.
A dragon feels soft.

Luca Christopher Bray (5)
Corbridge CE First School, Corbridge

Cat Senses Poem

Cats taste like fish with hair on.
It smells like fish.
It smells bad.
It looks cute and cuddly.
It feels soft and cuddly!

Anya De Gheldere (5)
Corbridge CE First School, Corbridge

Monkey Sense Poem

My monkey smells of hairy hair.
My monkey looks like a hairy dog.
My monkey sounds like ooo-aaa.
My monkey feels like a kitten.

Callum Charlton (5)
Corbridge CE First School, Corbridge

Polar Bear Sense Poem

Polar bears taste icy.
Polar bears smell icy.
Polar bears look snowy.
Polar bears sound grrrrrr.
Polar bears feel fluffy.

George McNally (5)
Corbridge CE First School, Corbridge

Yeti Sense Poem

Yeti tastes like meat.
Yeti smells like blackberries.
Yeti looks like snow.
Yeti sounds like a roar.
Yeti feels soft.

Harrison James Neal (6)
Corbridge CE First School, Corbridge

Crimp! Crimp! Crimp! Crimp!

C heeky, so cheeky!
R ustle, rustle in the grass.
I n the meadow in the sun,
M rs Crimp and the babies
P ouncing up and down having fun.

Lena Henderson (5)

Cranmere Primary School, Esher

The Goggly Nipper

He is as smelly as a big bog monster
which is made out of mud.
He is as scared as springy rabbits
jumping around.
He is as fast as a polka-dotted leopard
spreading around.
He is as big as Big Daddy stomping around.
He is as cheeky as a cheeky monkey
throwing banana skins everywhere!
He is as playful as a cat getting distracted
with a red light.
He is cleverer than a giraffe munching on
carrots all day long.
He is as soft as a lion's mane with a
feisty roar.

Daisy Armstrong (6)

Croftlands Infant School, Ulverston

The Guinea Pig That Only Ate Yellow Peppers

It barely drinks its water
like a cheeky monkey,
not stopping to drink water.
It is very nocturnal like a hanging
upside-down bat.
It climbs to the top of her house
just like her silly young twin.
It hates being carried about
like a big, barking dog.
It is as furry as a big lion's mane.
It nibbles my clothes
like a white cuddly rabbit.
It likes to have warm hugs like a cushion.
It speaks to be softly just like a real human.

Lily Joy Oakley (7)
Croftlands Infant School, Ulverston

The Whisky Cat

She sleeps up on the high hill
as high as a hilly mountain.
She goes hunting for greedy foxes
as creepy as mice.
She gobbles fish like lightning
and lots of milk to get more.
She sleeps day and night
as cosy as can be.
She purrs so loudly she wakes everyone up.
Her tail swishes until her tail gets tired.

Evie Robinson (6)
Croftlands Infant School, Ulverston

Charley The Cheeky Crocodile

He is as scaly as a snake.

He is as sly as a monkey.

He is as scary as a dinosaur.

He strikes his prey as fast as lightning.

He sparkles in the sunlight.

He slithers like a lizard.

He bathes in the slimy pond.

He snaps his mouth with his sharp teeth.

He smells of frog spawn.

Heather Dent (7)
Croftlands Infant School, Ulverston

The Naughty Cheetah

She runs far like a cat,
She likes to eat a chicken,
She likes to run as fast as a cheery tiger,
She is as sneaky as a prowling lion,
She is scary like a big, hungry lion,
Her claws are as sharp as a lion's claw,
Her teeth are as sharp as a lion's teeth.

Isla Brett (6)
Croftlands Infant School, Ulverston

The Sneaky Panda

He's as clever and amazing as an anteater.
He swipes his prey as quick as a flash.
He stomps around as loud as an elephant.
He likes to play as kind as can be.
He likes to travel up hills
and down as careful as he can be.
He snuggles as tight as he can.

Harrison Stringer (7)
Croftlands Infant School, Ulverston

Freddie The Cool Cheetah

He's as cool as a roller skater.

He is as big as a table.

He is as nice as a unicorn.

He is as fast as a super strike of lightning.

He likes to play tig with his prey.

He's as cute as a dog.

He is the coolest cheetah in the forest.

Isaac Couzens (7)

Croftlands Infant School, Ulverston

Life Of A Leopard Gecko

A leopard gecko is as spotty as a
Dalmatian.
He hides in the dirty rocks
like a plane in the fluffy clouds.
The leopard gecko leaps out on his prey
as fast as a Lamborghini.
He likes deserts as hot as red, flowing lava.

Jay Zahore (6)
Croftlands Infant School, Ulverston

Unicorns Are Magic

She is as magical as a rainbow.
She is as colourful as a rainbow.
She is as glittery as glitter.
She is as clever as a brain.
She is as soft as a feather.

Skye Elizabeth Joy Wilkinson Marsh (7)
Croftlands Infant School, Ulverston

Perfect Penguin To Finlay

He is soft like a pillow.

He is the best at sliding on ice.

He is the most cuddliest.

He is the best penguin.

He stomps like an elephant.

Finlay Cooper (6)

Croftlands Infant School, Ulverston

My Friend The Ant

This is a poem about my friend, the ant.
He is quite unusual because he wears pants!
He's got wheels for legs and a bell on
his tail
And his best friend isn't an ant - he's a snail!
My friend the ant is very good at gym -
He can lift a weight nearly as big as him!
One thing I know - and I'm sure you'll think
I'm lying -
My friend the ant is really good at flying!

Natasha Bloom (5)

Edge Grove School, Watford

The Fast Cheetah!

The cheetah, fierce in nature,
Swift like a flash as it goes by,
With its graceful fur swishing side to side.

The cheetah, a hungry predator,
Always hunting for its lunch,
Its favourite food is gazelle,
That it finds on the savannah.

The cheetah, a prince among all beasts.
Respected by flocks, feared by cubs,
It is speedy like a car,
Always one step ahead.

Dara Olunloyo (7)
Edge Grove School, Watford

The Cat And The Toroolos

There was one cat walking down the street
He found an apple tree
And ate 100 apples
And went back to his home.
There was one toroolos
Walking down the lane
And it saw an apple tree
And ate 100 apples
And he felt sick.
He went back to his home
And fell asleep
Until his mum woke him up.

Jessica Shah (6)
Edge Grove School, Watford

Rosie Unicorn Horsey

Rosie Unicorn Horsey loves to fly.
Her favourite place is in the sky.
Her horn makes magic and rainbows so
bright,
The sky is full of beautiful light.

Her hooves of gold glow in the night.
She really is a wonderful sight.
She munches and crunches her apples all
day,
And goes to sleep on a bed of hay.

Bryony Sanders (5)
Edge Grove School, Watford

Camels Are Mammals

One day sitting on a hunchback camel
And riding on a big back mammal.
Clumsy camels you find here and there,
Where do they go?
In grassy fields galloping greedily
for green grass.
Bumpy and lumpy camels race across
the silky sand.
Camels are mammals,
They're warm-blooded just like us.

Fatemah Asaria
Edge Grove School, Watford

The Cheetah Bug's Day

Cheetah Bug, Cheetah Bug
Flying through the jungle
As fast as you can.
Cheetah Bug, Cheetah Bug
Eating as many leaves as you can.
You are small but fast
As you fly through the jungle.
With your spotty back and big wings
You fly away to the beach.
Happy holidays.

Aisha Lawton (5)
Edge Grove School, Watford

Lion World

Roar! I am the lion who fights fiercely.
I have a scary face
And can beat anyone when I run.
The little boys cry when I catch them
And when I eat them
They taste like chocolate,
Yum! Yum! Yum!
Here I come to catch you!
Roar!

Yousuf Usmani (5)
Edge Grove School, Watford

Hoover The Hippo

Hoover the hippo lives in the zoo.
He poos in his pool
And his pool is his loo!
Cabbages are his best food.
He hoovers them up when he's in the mood.
They hide underwater so they don't
get eaten.
Nobody can beat Hoover when he's eating.

Freddie Mills-Webb (5)
Edge Grove School, Watford

Leopards

I see them far and near,
One of the most fierce animals.
They live in forests
And play in the mountains.
They can run faster than most animals.
Their spots are black as a crayon.
Their jaws are as sharp as a knife.
Leopards are as fierce as a lion.

Ehije Izzi-Engbeaya
Edge Grove School, Watford

The Elephant

There was an elephant called Oliver
Who liked to splash in water.
His friends came to play one day
And they splashed
And squirted water in a spray.
They had fun and slept in the sun
And the next day they went again.

Oliver Cox (5)
Edge Grove School, Watford

The Giraffe Poem

Long neck, small bum!
Tiny horns, blue tongue.
Skinny legs, crazy fur.
Taller than everyone!

India Bulmer (5)
Edge Grove School, Watford

Furry, Cheeky Creature

I am very, very cheeky.
I have a long, curly tail to wrap around the knees.
I have wide blue eyes to look at you.
I am very cute.
I like to swing from the trees like crazy.
I eat loads of bananas.
I live in the jungle but can you find me?
I love to climb the trees very quickly.
I have little pink ears for hearing you.
I love tricking people and having fun.
What am I?
I am a monkey!

Saachi Rajani (6)
Greenfield School, Woking

The Scariest In The World

He's as scary as a dragon.
He always wants to slither.
He loves to sneak up on other animals.
He loves to eat his prey:
Pigs, birds and mice.
He is mean as a lion and hyena.
He is as long as the longest
And tallest in the world.
You will always find him in the trees.
He will always roar at you.
He is the best you will see.
He has two heads.
He is a lion slither.

Austin Frith
Greenfield School, Woking

The Mighty Creeper

It has a long, yellow neck
like a yellow snake.
It has a green, long, crocodile tail
like a prickly cactus.
It has shiny, silver rocket boosters
like shiny silver coins.
It has silver, shiny boots like axes.
It likes to eat dog food, pizza
and ice cream for lunch.
He likes to go to Legoland and Disneyland.
He likes to play video games.
He is a mite creeper.

Matthew Denison-Edson

Greenfield School, Woking

The Deadly Zoo Animals

He is red, blue, green and yellow
like a mythical eagle.
He breathes fire like a fierce dragon.
He can hear from a million miles away.
He eats leopards, unicorns, baboons
and snakes.
He lives in the jungle because not many
Animals can eat him or scare him.
He lives in space
because he can lay eggs there.
What is he?

Vikram Kurup
Greenfield School, Woking

Owl

It is soft and cute, it can fly
And its wings are fuzzy.
It likes to do somersaults
And it likes bananas, carrots
And my lipgloss.
It lives in the woods
And it likes to come to my house.
It is cute and it likes to get friends.
It has soft, cuddly wings
And its name is Cuddly.
It's an owl!

Myeesha Amani Zaki (7)
Greenfield School, Woking

The Creature Who Ate Bananas

She has a big, brown tummy like a bear.
She has long arms like an elephant's trunk.
She has a bright red bow
Like the colour of strawberries.
She has two big ears like a human.
She has a bright white tail like the silver moon.
She has two big feet like slippers.
What is she?
She is a monkey!

Meng-Yao Ai
Greenfield School, Woking

Dragon

It flies as high as a bird.
It's as scary as an orange tiger.
Its tail is as long as a table.
Its wings are as colourful as the rainbow.
It's as tall as a long house.
It makes me feel scared as a dragon,
Blowing fire out of his nostrils.
It's a dragon.

Omar Elsharkawy
Greenfield School, Woking

The Monster Of The Sea

He has sharp teeth like a dinosaur.
He has eyes the colour of grass.
His skin is smooth and grey like a dolphin.
He likes to eat things like dolphins,
Fish, crabs and people.
He lives in the sea.
He likes to go everywhere.
He is a shark.

Harry Charlton (6)
Greenfield School, Woking

Trapdoor Spider

It's as hairy as a gorilla.

It waits as patiently as a boring poodle.

It walks on the ceiling like a gecko.

It has eyes like a scary monster.

It has fangs as sharp as a Komodo dragon.

It's a trapdoor spider.

Ruben Kalliopuska (7)

Greenfield School, Woking

The Giraffe

It is as long as a limousine.
Its legs are as skinny as a runner bean.
Its feet look like it's got a horseshoe.
Its ears are as sharp as a cat's ear.
Its nose looks ahead like a triangle.
It's a giraffe.

Inaya Kahn
Greenfield School, Woking

Untitled

When he flaps his wings he is faster than a
cheetah.
His fins are more spiky than splinters.
He shoots fire from his mouth like a
barbecue.
He is more vicious than a shark.
He lives at the bottom of the ocean.

Zachariah Placide-De-Horn
Greenfield School, Woking

Flying Blue Whale

It's as blue as the sea.
It likes to eat killer whales.
It likes to go to the city of New York.
It has seven eyes and four wings.
It makes me feel small.
It's a flying blue whale.

Jacob Jennings
Greenfield School, Woking

Bunny

It's as white as a snowball.
Its nose is as twitchy as a flea.
Its ears are very floppy.
It likes to nibble and dribbles.
It curls up in the hay.
It's a super bunny.

Daniel Tate
Greenfield School, Woking

The Horse Who Is A Rockstar

It's got colourful wings like a rainbow.
It's got a tail as fluffy as a bunny.
It's got big ears like a cauliflower.
It flies as high as a bird.
My horse, Daisy.

Darragh Dailey (6)
Greenfield School, Woking

Mountain Monster

He can swim like a fish.
He can climb like a monkey.
He has sharp claws like knives.
He's as friendly as a friend.
What is he?
He is an Alaskan bear.

Madeleine Chesher (7)
Greenfield School, Woking

The Skater

She has wide white eyes
She has a grey unicorn horn
She has brown wobbly wings
She throws pickles like a ball hitting a target
She eats red, soft cactus.

Mason Patrick Bartholomew (7)
Greenfield School, Woking

Loch Ness

It is as scary as a dragon,
It's as rare as a diamond,
It's as fearsome as a lion,
Its teeth are as sharp as a needle,
It's Nessie!

Oscar Elam
Greenfield School, Woking

Bunny

It's as white as snow.
It has a tail of snowballs.
It has long ears as long as tree trunks.
It really likes to eat carrots.
It is a bunny!

Anna Lucia Stempel-Martinez (6)
Greenfield School, Woking

Monkey Trouble

M onkeys eat bananas, they swing high up in trees all day and eat all day!

O ne sunny day he hides up in shady trees until the sun has gone away!

N o other monkey sleeps like him, he doesn't go to sleep until he snores!

K ing monkeys don't, they don't even snore! They just dream and dream until the morning!

E normous bananas are the best but they're very rare!

Y esterday he ate in the trees so much and banged his knees.

Lily Dolan (6)
Heather Avenue Infant School, Norwich

Kitten Life

K itten was very fun but very cheeky upon my tongue

I love my kitten, like lots of food. What do you like?

T iky Toky my kitten likes to play

T oo low, my kitten is proud

E njoying dinner, phew!

N ow what? You are hungry. Just for one day have your dinner at lunch. Here you go, what a day kitten. What a day! No more or you'll be sick!

Kara Rae Morgan (6)
Heather Avenue Infant School, Norwich

Naughty Monkey

My monkey likes to climb
And he drinks lime.
My monkey likes to sleep at night,
He sometimes wakes up in a fright.
He prowls through trees sometimes,
He gets stung by bees.
My monkey eats bananas and snails
But sometimes hurts his tail.
My monkey's everyone's friend
But sometimes ends up
Sending them around the bend.

Jake David Lofty (6)
Heather Avenue Infant School, Norwich

Fierce, Aggressive Tiger

I am hairy.
I am yellow, orange and red.
I kill and eat meat.
I love to be king.
I love to make friends
And love to fight with my friends.
I live in the jungle.
I love to practise my roars
And especially to practise with my Dad,
It is quite fun.
I starred in the Lion King.
What am I?

Emilis Galdikas (6)
Heather Avenue Infant School, Norwich

Darkness Is A Colour

She is used to moonlight,
if she sees a dash of light
she might get quite a fright!
My bat isn't fancy like a waistcoat.
My bat isn't friends with another bat,
she actually is with another cat.
Some people think my bat
looks like scary mice
but I think she looks pretty nice.

Kitty Clitheroe (7)
Heather Avenue Infant School, Norwich

Cheetah Facts

Cheetahs are fast and they never come last.
They hurt large zebras by jumping and thumping.
Cheetahs enjoy eating meat and cheese.
It runs and eats buns.
It kills to pay the bills.
Cheetahs are the fastest animals on the Planet Earth
And have a cub when they give birth.

Joel Ruane (7)
Heather Avenue Infant School, Norwich

The Monkey

There was a monkey
who stole a banana from a donkey.
He needed some food
because he was in a bold wood.
He swung through the trees
to have some leaves
And he got back to the tree
with his banana leaves
to eat for his dinner with his donkey.

Zaki Mokhbi (6)

Heather Avenue Infant School, Norwich

The Giraffe Path

My giraffe likes to run right through the sun.
My giraffe likes to play all through the day.
He likes to play in the forest
But not with his brother, Morris.
My giraffe is my best friend
Because he's fun
And never lets it end.

Finn Harrison (7)
Heather Avenue Infant School, Norwich

Scary Snake

S nake around in trees eating flesh do you please?

N agging at all the animals he sees

A sking for more food to eat

K eeping all of his scales clean and green

E ating scared, tiny mice with a big toothy grin.

Mya-Rose Moss (6)

Heather Avenue Infant School, Norwich

The Tiger

My animal has four legs.
My animal eats meat.
My animal likes to sleep.
My animal has an orange body.
My animal has stripes, they are black.
What am I?

Tanvir Singh Rakkar (7)

Heather Avenue Infant School, Norwich

What Am I?

I have a sharp beak.
I live in the freezing cold.
I love the snow.
I can catch fish.
I can waddle.
I am black and white.
What am I?

Ella Cudden (7)
Heather Avenue Infant School, Norwich

What Am I?

I have four legs.
I have short fur.
I eat grass.
I live in the jungle.
I have black and white stripes.
What am I?

Ivy Jean Philbrock (5)
Heather Avenue Infant School, Norwich

Mr Lion

Mr Lion, so big and strong,
How I like to hear you roar all day long.
You like to bathe in the sun
And chase animals just for fun.
You are King of the Jungle
But wear no crown.
Your mane is of magnificent, golden brown.
You are the fiercest animal around.

Darcey Elizabeth Copley (6)
Meynell Community Primary School, Sheffield

About Snow Leopards

Shy and secretive, never shows off
But obviously beautiful, wonderful at jumping.
Lives in the Himalayas,
Even on the rocky slopes.
One of the most endangered,
Patterned with spots,
Amazing, smart, really big tail.
Delightfully stunning to look at.

Majid Amponsem (6)
Meynell Community Primary School, Sheffield

The Spooky Cat Of The Jungle

Once there was a cat
That tried to hurt a bat.
The cat also tried to eat the rat.
The rat ran away from the cat.
Wherever there was a mouse,
You would find the cat outside his house.
But once the cat was sleepy,
He would return home, to the warm.

Amy Hobson (6)
Meynell Community Primary School, Sheffield

Hedgehog

Hedgehog, hedgehog
He's a nice one.
He's a shy one.
He's a cute one.
He's a spiky one.
He's a small one.
Hedgehog, hedgehog,
He's a stretchy one.

John Southhall (6)
New Leaf Inclusion Centre, Walsall

Dinosaur

Dinosaur with pink skin.
Dinosaur with yellow spots.
Dinosaur eats people.
Dinosaur in a cave.
Dinosaur in the city.
Dinosaur in an igloo.
Dinosaur might eat you!

Sophie Byrne (5)
New Leaf Inclusion Centre, Walsall

Snake, Snake, Snake

Snake, snake, snake
Colourful skin
Slithering silently
Swallowing superbly
Straight and slimy
Snake, snake, snake.

Brayden Tyrese Francis (6)
New Leaf Inclusion Centre, Walsall

Crocduck

Walking slowly
Quacking scarily
Swimming quietly
Eating loudly
Sharp teeth snapping fiercely
Crocduck!

Joshua Jay Till (6)
New Leaf Inclusion Centre, Walsall

Hedgehog

H edgehogs sleep in winter
E very day they scurry across the road
D on't like the cold
G ood at curling up when scared
E xcited for summer
H edgehogs are as brown as a tree trunk
O nly likes to eat wiggly worms
G ot spikes as sharp as an alligator's teeth.

Francesca Brett (6)
Oakhill School, Clitheroe

Alligator

A lligators are fierce

L ong spikes

L ong whacking tail

I think alligators are as green as a leaf

G oing into the horrible water

A lligators are a wet animal

T eeth as sharp as a knife

O m nom nom when it eats people

R eady to fight!

George Purves (6)
Oakhill School, Clitheroe

About Giraffes

G iraffes' necks are as long as an elephant's trunk

I n Africa is where they live

R eally long legs

A giraffe has wobbly legs like a jelly

F ur as yellow as a banana

F un to watch

E ars as small as a mouse.

Isabella Zappa (6)
Oakhill School, Clitheroe

Cheeky Gorilla

G orillas are as black as an

O ctopus' ink

R ound, shiny eyes

I s as cheeky as me!

L oud grunts

L ong hairy arms for climbing trees

A nose as flat as a pancake.

George Crook (5)
Oakhill School, Clitheroe

Tiger Stripes

T igers are as loud as the school bell
I n the jungle is where they live
G rumpy and angry
E nergetic, fast and strong
R acing orange and black stripes.

Evan Black (6)
Oakhill School, Clitheroe

Rabbit

R abbits have big, black eyes

A s fluffy as a cat

B ig pink ears

B ushy tail

I t jumps really high

T eeny, tiny rabbit.

Elysia Blackburn (5)

Oakhill School, Clitheroe

Lion

L ions are as furry as a cat
I n the jungle they eat animals
O n their heads is a big bushy mane
N obody would survive without a lion.

Thomas Ashworth (6)
Oakhill School, Clitheroe

Dog

D ogs are as soft as a rabbit's belly
O utside a dog loves to play
G ot fur as brown as chocolate.

Orlaith Purves (6)

Oakhill School, Clitheroe

Foxes

F oxes are as orange as a sunset
O utside foxes pounce
E xtraordinary animals.

Caspar Cort (6)
Oakhill School, Clitheroe

Cat, Cat

C ats are cute
A s furry as a jumper
T ail is as stripy as a tiger.

Katie Hennighan (5)
Oakhill School, Clitheroe

Shana The Llama Farmer

Shana the llama lived on a farm, with a
sheep and a pig and a horse in a barn
They all were looked after by Larry the
farmer, who they all loved so much
especially Shana
Larry the farmer loved his llama, he brushed
her fur every day.
Shana the llama loved the farmer, but one
day he went away
The sheep needed grass, the horse needed
hay, they all wished Larry had never gone
away.
Shana helped where she could whilst time
did pass, she found the pig new mud and
for the sheep some new grass.
Then one day they heard the noise of a car,
they ran to the gate to peer through the
bar.
There he stood at the door to the farm with
a bandage on his head and a broken arm.

He spotted his animals and they grunted with joy
He was here, he was back
Their favourite boy.
They helped him get well day after day, they all were so happy he was back to stay.
Hip hip hooray!

Chloe Isabella Greenway (6)
Priorslee Academy, Telford

Leaping Leopard

Leopards in books mainly sleep but mine likes to leap!
When I brush my leopard's fur it leaps with a lot of sound,
It makes me go backwards and fall to the ground.
When I put it in a cage, it bursts out and attacks like a sabre-toothed tiger from Ice Age.
Its long, wiry whiskers poke me on the arm,
I always tell my mum but she tells me to remain calm.
My leaping leopard likes to explore and run but it always eats my honey buns!
I see its sharp teeth baring at me but I love the leopard and the leaping leopard loves me!
Well as far as I can see.

Sian Kaur Hothi (7)
Priorslee Academy, Telford

My Little Panda

My little panda is soft and furry
My little panda is happy and blurry
Today my little panda wants to play and
play until night
One sunny day, my little panda saw a rustle
in the bushes
She saw two yellow eyes which gleamed in
the sun
She saw four orange legs
It was not a bear because it had a white-
tipped tail
My little panda was afraid it was a monster
But it wasn't a monster, instead it was a fox
My little panda was scared because its only
enemy was fox
She ran away as fast as she could and she
never went there again.

Aditi Singla (6)
Priorslee Academy, Telford

Jaguar, Jaguar

Jaguar, jaguar, where can you be,
I've looked all around but cannot see.
Can you roar to give me a clue,
Then I will be able to find you?
Jaguar, jaguar, where can you be,
Are you hiding behind a tree?
If it's food that you need, then I can provide
But really I assure you there's no reason to
hide.
Jaguar, jaguar, are you trapped in a cage,
Is that why you scream and roar with rage?
'No!' said the big cat. 'It's not really me,
I'm not a jaguar but a cheetah you see.'

Freya Faye Harris (7)
Priorslee Academy, Telford

Monkeys

I think monkeys
Are rather funky
Their tails are long
Their nose looks wrong
But their ears are right
And their teeth are white

I think monkeys
Are rather furry
Their bodies are hairy
Apart from their face
Which is pink and scary

I think monkeys
Are rather naughty
On trees they swing
And they steal people's things
That they shouldn't touch
But I still like them very much.

Mahi Patel
Priorslee Academy, Telford

Cheetahs

Padded paws strike the ground
Who might these paws belong to?
A cheetah of course, chasing its prey
But it has given up now
Lying in the shade under the trees
Now seeks another prey, what could this prey be?
It was a little mouse, it was only little but it would do for now
It was time to rest, time for peace in the rainforest...
At least for a little bit
There were night animals that lurked in the dark
Such as bats and tree frogs.

Eva Clayton (6)
Priorslee Academy, Telford

Ocelots

An ocelet can be shy but is it a scaredy cat
or a furry cat?
They are very spotty, it must make them
potty
All day they hunt and play
And all night they sleep tight
It hides in the grass waiting for lunch to
walk past.

Thomas Faulkner (6)
Priorslee Academy, Telford

My Super Polar Bear

My polar bear likes to sleep outside in a
cave
In the dark he has to be very brave
He saves everybody from scary things
And makes people happy when he sings
My super polar bear.

Brooke Smith (5)
Priorslee Academy, Telford

The Panther's Life

There strolls a panther cold in the night,
It's sharp, dangerous teeth are seen in the bright,
Down by the riverbank where everything glows,
It catches its prey wherever it goes.

James Frederick Atwell (6)

Priorslee Academy, Telford

The Sharkanda

The sharkanda is...
As mean as a troll
As big as a lamp post
As silly as my brother
As good as my teacher
As clever as my teacher
As scared as me
As hungry as the head teacher
As happy as my dad
And as quiet as my mum.

Hefin Salisbury (7)
Scholar Green Primary School, Stoke-On-Trent

The Pupit

The pupit is as cuddly as a teddy bear
As kind as a mouse
As friendly as me
As small as a button
As happy as a clown
As hairy as a lion
And dirty like a farmyard.

Lily Viner (7)
Scholar Green Primary School, Stoke-On-Trent

The Dragolion

The dragolion is...
As scaly as a snake
As big as an elephant
As clever as a leopard
As fast as lightning
As strong as a metal mansion
And as friendly as a cat.

Darcey Rose Yarwood (6)
Scholar Green Primary School, Stoke-On-Trent

The Spicroc

The spicroc is...
As green as a football pitch
As mean as a dragon
As fast as a car
As big as a tree
As friendly as a tiger
And as soft as a snake.

Ethan Morris (6)
Scholar Green Primary School, Stoke-On-Trent

The Dobbit

The dobbit is...
Fluffy as a pillow
As kind as my friend
As happy as can be
As big as a child
As fast as a cheetah
And as friendly as a dog.

Lola Thornton (7)
Scholar Green Primary School, Stoke-On-Trent

The Puptig

My animal is...
Soft as a cloud
Nice as a dog
Fast as a car
Small as a pet
Loud as an elephant
Warm as a fire
And as funny as can be.

Sally Beatrice Knight (7)
Scholar Green Primary School, Stoke-On-Trent

The Snird

The snird is...
As small as a mouse
As kind as my dog
As green as the grass
As sad as my pillow
And his legs are smarter than a pencil.

Darcie Gannon (7)
Scholar Green Primary School, Stoke-On-Trent

The Skird

The skird is...
As mean as a crocodile
As fast as a Ferrari
As clever as a sly fox
As big as a boulder
And is stronger than a brick.

William Hough (7)
Scholar Green Primary School, Stoke-On-Trent

The Scail

My animal is...
Mean as a shark
It is as greedy as a pig
It is as slow as a sniper
It is as suspicious as a tiger
He likes to hunt.

Roan Hercock (6)
Scholar Green Primary School, Stoke-On-Trent

The Lunicorn

The Lunicorn is...
As kind as a mouse
As big as a car
As thoughtful as me
As magical as a wizard
And as soft as my best teddy.

Mara Taylor-Woods (7)
Scholar Green Primary School, Stoke-On-Trent

The Cowse

The cowse is...
As generous as me
As tall as Miss Hope
As heavy as my dad
As furry as my cat
And my friend.

Dainton Skot Frost (7)

Scholar Green Primary School, Stoke-On-Trent

Anspid

My animal is anspid
It is mean as a rodent
It is small like a beetle
It likes to eat meat
Greedy like a pig.

Nicholas Davies (6)
Scholar Green Primary School, Stoke-On-Trent

The Eleraffe

My animal is...
Nice as a dog
Tall as a tower
Greedy as a cat
Faster than a cheetah
Brave as a tiger.

Molly Norbury (7)
Scholar Green Primary School, Stoke-On-Trent

The Spifis

My animal is...
Mean as a lion
As soft as a spider
Crazy as Mum
As small as a fish
He likes to run.

Shaun Cavanagh-Frost (6)
Scholar Green Primary School, Stoke-On-Trent

The Scorpull

My animal is...
Fast as a cheetah
It has horns to eat his prey
It likes to sleep
It likes to eat deer.

Thomas Lewis (7)

Scholar Green Primary School, Stoke-On-Trent

The Unipig

My animal is...
As fast as lightning
As mean as a bull
As weird as a pig
As tall as a mountain.

Noah Cole (7)
Scholar Green Primary School, Stoke-On-Trent

It Is Called Scorpark

My animal is...
Mean as a robber
As quick as a car
As scary as a knife
A good predator.

Joseph Oliver (7)
Scholar Green Primary School, Stoke-On-Trent

The Grafhorse

My animal is...
Faster than a human
Bigger than my teacher.

Evie Potts (6)
Scholar Green Primary School, Stoke-On-Trent

Fox Mistakes All Day

Underneath the dark, damp, underground hideout,
The fox snores louder than an elephant blowing blue books,
He catches his prey, like a flash of lightning,
He dashes to Treasure Land to find his mother's marvellous, make-up,
The fox goes to Friend Zone to make new friends every day,
He ends up at Lazy House to sleep the night away.

Lauren Thompson (7)

St James Catholic Primary School, Millom

Panda Poem!

A panda in a heap of leaves is very lazy.
She likes to go to the bamboo shop.
She buys beautiful, bouncy, blue bamboo
shoots to decorate her house.
She goes underneath a huge shoot of
bamboo to sleep like a newborn baby.
When she wakes she eats like a hungry
hippo.

Bella Pedley (7)
St James Catholic Primary School, Millom

Bamboo Panda

By the grey, hard cave there lived a grey,
white and black panda
It catches its prey as fast as a butterfly
fluttering about
She goes to the bamboo bear for her tea
and her dinner
At the end of the day she goes under a tree
and sleeps there all night.

Maya Clarke (6)
St James Catholic Primary School, Millom

All About Kitties

I have a cat called Jessy
Jessy has a sister called Bessy
Jessy likes to eat fresh fishy
From her purple pawed dishy
She lives in a flat near Nottingham
But my grandma lives in Cottingham
She's sweet, she's kind and pretty
What a lovely little kitty!
When she visits me it's a pity
She leaves the carpet bitty
What a messy Jessy!

Martha Elizabeth Needler (6)

St John Of Beverley RC Primary School, Beverley

The Secret Life Of Rainbowguineasheep

My rainbowguineasheep is woolly, fluffy and colourful
She smells like rainbows and stars
She likes to hide inside her cage
Her favourite place is under her bed
When she is scared she moves like a snake...
And when she is happy she skips like a butterfly.

Sarah Gibson (6)

St John's CE Primary School, Sandbach

Kian The Lion

A lion is smelly, sometimes rude and silly
He always tells jokes, ha ha ha!
He hides in his hiding place
And jumps out when people are not
expecting it
He stomps like an elephant through the
grass
And he jumps like a ginormous frog.

Lauren Jayne Ann Clorley (7)
St John's CE Primary School, Sandbach

The Fat Cat

My cat is fat, shy and funny
My cat is funny, happy and fluffy
She hides under her cushion because she
gets scared
My cat hides behind her bed
When my cat walks in the house like a dog,
the cat purrs
The cat's tail waves a lot.

Gemma Groves (7)
St John's CE Primary School, Sandbach

The Night Of The Living Hamster

A flying hamster goes to the shops
To buy her own food without paying
Then the knife goes *shshsh* on the toast
It hides in my pocket
And in St John's she flutters like a bird in the sky
But she might be in your home?

Oscar Alexander Forsyth (7)

St John's CE Primary School, Sandbach

The Fat Sniken

A sniken is hilarious, friendly and handsome
A sniken is cool and selfish
He lives underground in meerkat tunnels
He can find a wife very easily underground
He slithers in the meerkat tunnels like a mouse
He eats like a bird.

Xanthe Williams (6)
St John's CE Primary School, Sandbach

Miffy The Owlet

An owlet is brown, round and fluffy
An owlet smells grassy
My owlet soars on top of trees looking for
food
An owlet hides around trees
Miffy the owlet hides in trees like a monkey
Owls peck at food like a bird.

Alyssa Calladine (7)
St John's CE Primary School, Sandbach

The Muddy Pig

A pig is muddy, smelly and smooth
sometimes
Pigs are nice, friendly and clean
He hides behind a fence to spy on the
farmer
The piggy is splashing in mud
He jumps in mud like a bear
He is muddy like a cow.

Jasmine Briggs (7)
St John's CE Primary School, Sandbach

Bobbly Shark

My dragon is big and scary
He is called Bobbly and is always hungry
He hides under the rocks
And sometimes in his cave
He swims in the sea
He breathes fire like a candle
He stomps like an elephant.

Jeff-Lewis Cook (7)
St John's CE Primary School, Sandbach

My Horse Betty

My horse is fast, black and soft
It is big, tall and long
She sits down when it rains
She likes hiding behind hay bales
It runs fast like a cheetah when it moves
It eats like a cow and is always hungry.

Mieke Marie Douglas (7)
St John's CE Primary School, Sandbach

The Poem Of Cats!

A cat is furry, cute and fun to play with
Happy, smiley and black
He likes to hide under a cave
He plays underneath his cage
He runs like a cheetah through the grass
He also runs like a leopard.

Iona Acir (7)
St John's CE Primary School, Sandbach

The Snaffe

A snaffe is strange, long and slithery
A snaffe is spotty, friendly and cute
She hides under gaps
She hides behind tall trees
She slithers like a fish in the sea
She smiles like a friendly girl.

Amelia Mitchell (6)
St John's CE Primary School, Sandbach

The Snake Slither

My snake is slimy, big and fast
Every time he plays tag he never ever gets
tagged
He hides under some big sticks
Every time he plays hide-and-seek
He slithers like a worm in the long grass.

Joseph Hollins (6)
St John's CE Primary School, Sandbach

Amy The Cheetah

Amy looks spotty, fast and small
She eats snakes and fish
She lives inside a cave
She loves going around anything
She likes going super fast
She likes scaring other animals.

Ruby Musgrave (6)
St John's CE Primary School, Sandbach

The Prey Fish

My prey fish is scary and he eats fish
He is mean and hungry
He hides in the dark so he can eat them
He swims like an ant that's eating.

Archie Brennan (7)
St John's CE Primary School, Sandbach

Bigyosaurus

The bigyosaurus is big and scary
He is fierce when he is in a cave
He is funny like a fish.

Joseph Calladine (7)
St John's CE Primary School, Sandbach

Fish

My fish is a girl
She blows bubbles like an elephant
She likes to swim up the tree like a snake.

Kaitlyn Clee (6)
St John's CE Primary School, Sandbach

Goldfish

My fish is cute and colourful
Like a rainbow
My fish is funny and cute
Like a giraffe

Nicole Clee (6)

St John's CE Primary School, Sandbach

My Guinea Pig

My guinea pig likes climbing like a mouse
My guinea pig likes hiding like a snake.

Caitlin Levitt (6)
St John's CE Primary School, Sandbach

The Little Giraffe

The little giraffe was playing
The giraffe was saying hello to the fox
Who was singing
The giraffe was cute
The giraffe was picking a spot
The giraffe was walking around
The giraffe was making a sound.

Aasma Amna Khan (6)
Westwood Prep School, Oldham

Snakey

I love Snakey, he is slithering
His stinging is very hard
He hates rocks and elephants
And rabbits too
He loves cats
He's fast too
He is sharp.

Huzayfah Muhammad (6)
Westwood Prep School, Oldham

Cheetah

My cheetah is fast
My cheetah is lovely
My cheetah is ugly
My cheetah likes mice
My cheetah is nice
My cheetah is sleepy
My cheetah is sleeky.

Muhammad Ismail (6)
Westwood Prep School, Oldham

The Little Baby

The little baby was stuck
The little baby got out
He was brave
So he did not cry
The little one was cute
My tiger is a beaut.

Hannah Brown (6)
Westwood Prep School, Oldham

The Tiger

The little tiger, soft and fat
The little tiger is scary and sarcy
The tiger has sharp claws
The tiger likes to charm.

Fatimah AZ-Zahra Rasul (6)
Westwood Prep School, Oldham

The Mystic Firebird

With its fiery wings it shoots in the sky
It's really fast
So you can't see it fly
It sparkles like a firework and burns up your
homework
With wings like an eagle
And it thinks there's no such thing as an
beagle
It likes to eat fruit but it can't wear a suit
It doesn't like rain because it takes out the
flame
It's very rare and absolutely loves fairies
It's a mystic firebird.

Jackson Haiden Sheahan (7)
Wood End Primary School, Atherstone

My Imaginary Magical Pet

She is blue and violet like a dark snowy sky
Her eyes are bright green like emeralds that sparkle
Her blue tail swishes like a wave on the sea
Her unicorn horn glitters in the sun
She's friendly and cuddly and can fly really high
She lives in a tree and has lots of fun
She is my flying unicorn dragon
Her name is Honey Bun!

Phoebe Hardwick (7)
Wood End Primary School, Atherstone

The Teddy Bear Riddle

I have a furry body like a cuddly teddy bear
My favourite food is delicious human flesh
I worship a golden god
I live high up in the tall trees
My large eyes shine like jewels in the
shimmering moonlight
I am very wise and friendly
You can find me on the Forest Moon of
Endor
Who am I?

A: Ewok.

Florence Rose Kinson (7)
Wood End Primary School, Atherstone

My Favourite Animal

She frolics around like small children in
fields and woods
She loves to munch and crunch on hay all
day
She also loves to nibble on grass and
vegetables
She's as cute as a kitten
She hops away quickly from her predators
So that she doesn't get bitten
She is safe when she's snuggled down in her
burrow.

Georgina Flavell-Dodson (7)
Wood End Primary School, Atherstone

All About My Cat

In memory of my cats Mica and Leo, my best friends

He's as black as coal
He's as white as snow
He's as soft as feathers
He's as nice as angels
But can be grumpy as a lion
He's as fast as a leopard
He purrs when somebody strokes him
His tongue is rough like a brush
It's my cat 'Mica'.

Olivia Schall (7)
Wood End Primary School, Atherstone

She Is Beautiful

She is as beautiful as a flower
She likes to play outside and run about
She is as big as a tower
She eats big bales of hay and juicy green grass
She is as white as the snow
She lives in the lovely field and gallops about all day
She likes to stay out until the sun goes down.

Lily-May Connie Gleeson (7)
Wood End Primary School, Atherstone

Snow King

I'm as white as snow
I'm big and strong as a rock
I have a very big bite
My claws are sharp as crocodile's teeth,
My fur is as warm as the sun
I smell my food from miles away
My home is as cold as ice.

Lottie-Leigh Amiee Oattes (6)
Wood End Primary School, Atherstone

Rainbow Dogs

It's a fluffy as a cloud
She is as cute as a kangaroo
She's as funny as a clown
When it rains it lights up like a rainbow
She likes to jump like a rabbit
It's Poppy the dog.

Izabelle Maddison Carroll (7)
Wood End Primary School, Atherstone

G'day Mate

He's two foot tall and grey and white
He likes to munch his leaves alone
He clings onto a eucalyptus tree
G'day my Australian koala.

Euan Markgraaff (7)
Wood End Primary School, Atherstone

The Girorse

I am so tall you can't come near me
I am so fast I don't come last
My spots are so pretty
I love to run
It's so much fun
I am yellow, brown and black!

I love to be groomed or stroked
Don't come here or I'll kick you
I cannot talk or say, 'How do you do?'
You cannot see that I am pleased
I'll always be hitting!

Ava Dickeson (6)
Woodlea Primary School, Houghton Le Spring

It's A Blackbird

I'm black, yellow, red and blue
Don't look into my eyes
I can count down from ten
Then you'll be hypnotised
My favourite game is I-Spy
Because I zoom in with my eyes
I can see miles away
So my friends say bye-bye
I looked into the sea
I said, 'It was a ship.'
I am very crafty and sneaky
I ate their fish and chips.

Finley Pringle (7)
Woodlea Primary School, Houghton Le Spring

It's A Liobra

I love to run around
I'm the fastest in the land
My friend's always ask me
'Do you go around the bend?'

I'm black and white
I love to fly my kite
But more I love to play around
And eat you in one bite!
I love to eat things off trees
But some animals are bigger than me!

George William McDonald (6)
Woodlea Primary School, Houghton Le Spring

I Am A Crocophant

My skin is green
My back is scaly
I would eat you in a bite
I can swim softly
But when I come across someone
I don't swim anymore
Instead I lick my lips
I swallow him whole

I stamp, I'm big
I'm very loud
You must be very proud!

Jake Henry Shaw (7)
Woodlea Primary School, Houghton Le Spring

It's A Rabbger

I can bounce and touch a tree
My favourite food is carrots
I grab them out from the ground
I share them with my crab!

I can hide in a cave
I can jump out and scare people
I can pretend I am a monster
When things break
I get my tools and fix it.

Beau Edith Gritton (6)
Woodlea Primary School, Houghton Le Spring

It's An EagleOcto

My feathers are black and white
I'm sure of that, see!
I am as sticky as can be
I can fly up to the trees

I like to stick to the ground
My favourite game is ping pong
I will beat you any time
Watch out I can catch you with my beak.

Amelia Kelsey (6)
Woodlea Primary School, Houghton Le Spring

Untitled

My body is grey as can be
The greyest animal in the sea
If you look in my eye
You'll get a big surprise

I will give you a cup of tea
I'm scary, I can poison you
But only if you don't give me
My tasty cup of tea.

Jasmine Slack (7)
Woodlea Primary School, Houghton Le Spring

I'm A Mouseep

I am very grey and white and pink
I have a long tail with long whiskers
I have loads of fur
I'm like a cushion!

My plans are so good
All I do is eat grass
I will eat your pass!
I sing like I'm crazy
Why are you so bad?

Sophie Green (6)
Woodlea Primary School, Houghton Le Spring

I'm A Zebous

I'm stripy everywhere
I like to run about
I sometimes play in my cage
I can't wait until I get out!

I feed myself a lot
You're going to be my dinner
I'm faster than you
I'm going to be the winner!

Nathan Johnson (6)
Woodlea Primary School, Houghton Le Spring

Bearphant

My favourite game is tag
I reach up for food
My favourite place to go
Is the quiet place in the jungle

I snore really loudly
I wake up everyone
My favourite colour is purple
I'm now off for a run!

Eleanor Hall (6)
Woodlea Primary School, Houghton Le Spring

It's A Rabiger

I love to run about
To catch a tasty trout
I am grey, blue and black
Because I want to have a snack

I run about to catch my prey
You'll see me one day
I'm fast on my legs
To crush baby eggs.

Daniel Wells (6)
Woodlea Primary School, Houghton Le Spring

I'm An Octoear

I am blue and green and orange
I have four arms
I am very happy but lazy

I am very brown and scary
I like to watch my friends
I am a bear
I will tear you up
I am a bear
I love to eat rabbits.

Lily Greenwood (6)
Woodlea Primary School, Houghton Le Spring

I Am A Tigeraffe

My skin is yellow and spotty
My friends think I'm very tall
I have a very long neck
I am taller than a high wall

I'm very stripy, black and orange
I like to run fast
I never come last!

Grace Bell (7)
Woodlea Primary School, Houghton Le Spring

The Plake

My skin is pink and green
I am furry and long
I have lots of scales
But I feel soft
My favourite food is Sunday lunch
I really like to munch
My favourite game is to swim
In the deep blue sea.

Oliver Dodsworth (7)
Woodlea Primary School, Houghton Le Spring

It's A Girabra

I am bigger than a tree
I am black and white
My favourite game is tig
I love to mess about

I love to sleep all day and night
I love to run
I'm very fast
I'm never last!

Antoine Turnbull (7)
Woodlea Primary School, Houghton Le Spring

Logon

My fur is orange and peach
My claws are so sharp
You will never beat me

I have black stripes
So I can hide in the grass
I smell everything I go past
I go for a healthy walk!

Libby Bonner (6)
Woodlea Primary School, Houghton Le Spring

I'm A Giraffe

I am spotty and furry
I am orange and black
My skin is brown
My favourite game is tig

I have big feet
I love to eat a sausage
My favourite food is meat.

Jake O'Shaughnessy (6)
Woodlea Primary School, Houghton Le Spring

I'm A Girafion

I can stretch my neck to reach my food,
I reach up my neck to the trees
To see my prey.

I can see my prey from everywhere,
It's cool to be so tall.

Matthew Warwick (6)
Woodlea Primary School, Houghton Le Spring

Zebot

My skin is colourful and spotty
I have furry skin and it is stripy
I am orange, red, green and blue
It is pink, black and white
I have big feet.

Caitlyn Allsopp (6)
Woodlea Primary School, Houghton Le Spring

The Lion

Meat-eater
Zebra-catcher
Snored sleepily
At its den
Loud-roarer
Mane-shaker.

William Anderson-Bell (5)
Woodlea Primary School, Houghton Le Spring

The Tiger

Tree-scratcher
Meat-eater
Orange and black-striper
Land-dweller
Jungle-dweller.

Ava Maddison (6)
Woodlea Primary School, Houghton Le Spring

The Cat

Mouse-chaser
Dog-hater
Loud-snorer
Fast-runner
Couch-scratcher.

Millie Lumsdon (6)
Woodlea Primary School, Houghton Le Spring

The Lion

Meat-eater
Zebra-hunter
Sharp claw-scratcher
Loud-roarer
Mane-shaker.

Jay Marlow (6)
Woodlea Primary School, Houghton Le Spring

The Lion

Meat-eater
Zebra-hunter
Sharp claw-scratcher
Loud-snorer
Mane-shaker.

Alfie Halliwell (5)
Woodlea Primary School, Houghton Le Spring

The Lion

Meat-eater
Zebra-hater
Sharp claw-scratcher
Loud-roarer
Mane-shaker.

Jodie-Marie Corbett (5)
Woodlea Primary School, Houghton Le Spring

A Snake

Tail-flapper
Body-wriggler
Long-mover
Tongue-slitter
Scary-hisser.

Freddie Temple (6)

Woodlea Primary School, Houghton Le Spring

A Fish

Quick-swimmer
Fast-mover
Tail-flapper
Body-swisher
Water-breather.

Ethan James Suthern (5)

Woodlea Primary School, Houghton Le Spring

A Snake

Scary-hisser
Tail-wriggler
Tongue-sticker
Body-slider
Long-mover.

Jacob Patterson Brown (5)

Woodlea Primary School, Houghton Le Spring

A Dragon

Fire-breather
Scary-fighter
Sharp-clawer
Tail-wagger
Big-eater.

Matthew Kelters (6)

Woodlea Primary School, Houghton Le Spring

The Dog

Fast-runner
Tongue-licker
Tail-wagger
Park-digger
Cat-chaser.

Ben Richardson (6)
Woodlea Primary School, Houghton Le Spring

Unicorn

Fast-runner
High-flyer
Tail-swisher
Hay-eater
Magic-wisher.

Violet Worrall (5)

Woodlea Primary School, Houghton Le Spring

A Unicorn

High-flyer
Fast-runner
Tail-swisher
Hay-eater
Magic-wisher.

Megan Bell (5)
Woodlea Primary School, Houghton Le Spring

A Horse

Fast-runner
Hay-eater
Tail-swisher
Quick-trotter
Fun-rider.

Emelia Grace Hood (5)

Woodlea Primary School, Houghton Le Spring

The Lion

Zebra-hunter
Sharp claw-scratcher
Loud-roarer
Mane-shaker.

James B Hudson (5)

Woodlea Primary School, Houghton Le Spring

The Tiger

Roaring meat-eater
Orange and black striper
Jungle dweller.

Aaron Dye (6)

Woodlea Primary School, Houghton Le Spring

The Tiger

Meat eater
Sharp claw
Sharp teeth
Roar!

Oliver Nattrass (6)
Woodlea Primary School, Houghton Le Spring

The Tiger

Meat-eater

Grass-hider

Long-tail

Sharp teeth.

Liam Snowball (6)

Woodlea Primary School, Houghton Le Spring